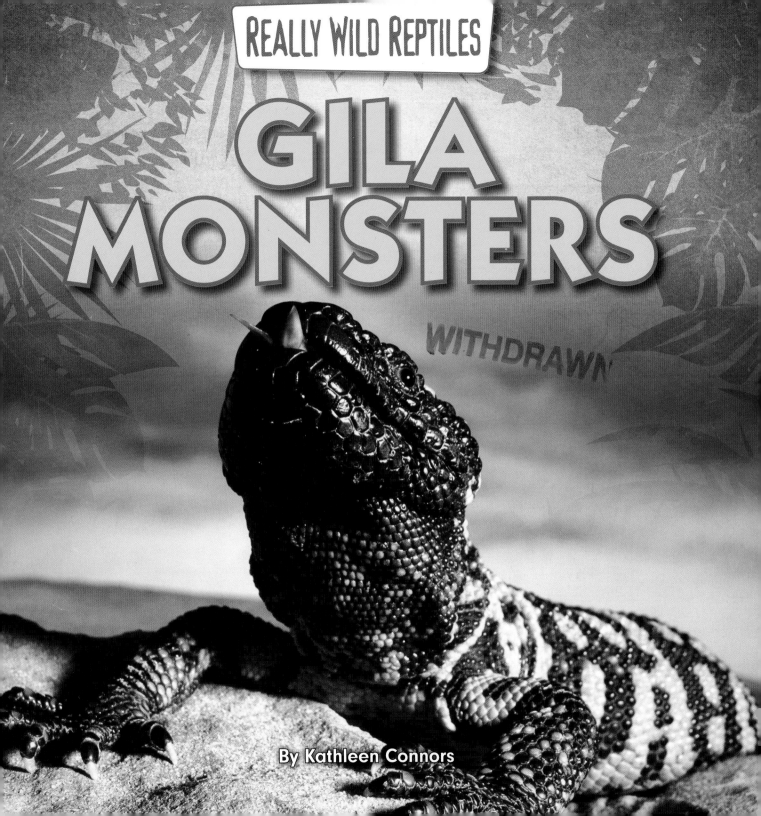

GILA MONSTERS

By Kathleen Connors

Please visit our website, www.garethstevens.com. For a free color catalog of all our high-quality books, call toll free 1-800-542-2595 or fax 1-877-542-2596.

Library of Congress Cataloging-in-Publication Data

Connors, Kathleen.
 Gila monsters / Kathleen Connors.
      p. cm. — (Really wild reptiles)
 Includes index.
 ISBN 978-1-4339-8370-2 (pbk.)
 ISBN 978-1-4339-8371-9 (6-pack)
 ISBN 978-1-4339-8369-6 (library binding)
 1. Gila monster—Juvenile literature. I. Title.
 QL666.L247C66 2013
 597.95'952—dc23

                                                  2012021878

First Edition

Published in 2013 by
Gareth Stevens Publishing
111 East 14th Street, Suite 349
New York, NY 10003

Designer: Ben Gardner
Editor: Kristen Rajczak

Photo credits: Cover, p. 1 Tim Flach/Stone/Getty Images; p. 5 © iStockphoto.com/Erik Bettini; p. 7 © iStockphoto.com/Christine Glade; p. 9 © iStockphoto.com/Prill Mediendesign & Fotografie; p. 11 Matt Jeppson/Shutterstock.com; pp. 13, 15 John Cancalosi/Peter Arnold/Getty Images; p. 17 C. Allan Morgan/Peter Arnold/Getty Images; p. 19 © iStockphoto.com/Bob Kupbens; p. 20 fivespots/Shutterstock.com; p. 21 Michael Kern/Visuals Unlimited/Getty Images.

Printed in the United States of America

CPSIA compliance information: Batch #CW13GS: For further information contact Gareth Stevens, New York, New York at 1-800-542-2595.

Contents

Words in the glossary appear in **bold** type the first time they are used in the text.

WHAT'S IN A NAME?

With such a wild name, you might guess that a Gila monster is a terrifying **predator**. They do have a **venomous** bite, but this lizard isn't all that scary. Gila monsters would rather hide underground than live up to their name.

Gila monsters are the largest lizards in North America. Like other **reptiles**, they're ectothermic, which means how hot or cold they are depends on how hot or cold their surroundings are. Read on for more cool facts!

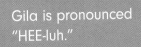

SCALE AND TAIL

Gila monsters have a big, heavy-looking body. They grow up to about 2 feet (60 cm) long and commonly weigh 3 to 5 pounds (1.4 to 2.3 kg). Gila monsters have a fat tail and small legs.

Most lizards are covered in flat scales, but not Gila monsters! Their skin is bumpy. It's made up of bead-like scales called osteoderms. Each scale has a small bone inside it. The scales are black or brown with brightly colored bands or spots.

What a Wild Life!
There are only two kinds of Gila monster: the reticulated Gila monster and the banded Gila monster.

Gila monsters are in a scientific group called Heloderma, which comes from Greek words meaning "studded skin."

KEEP OUT OF THE SUN

Gila monsters mainly live in Arizona and the deserts of the southwestern United States. They can be found in parts of New Mexico, Utah, Nevada, California, and northwestern Mexico.

Gila monsters spend as much as 90 percent of their life underground! They dig **burrows** with their sharp claws or use those made by other animals. Gila monsters commonly live in areas where there are plenty of rocks to hide under. These lizards don't want to be caught in the hot desert sun.

Because they spend so much time underground, it's not common to see a Gila monster.

What a Wild Life!

Gila monsters are named for the Gila River Basin found in Arizona and a small part of New Mexico.

Gila monsters are most active in the springtime. That's when they **mate** and are able to find lots of food. For the rest of the year, gila monsters spend much of their time alone.

Gila monsters move slowly around their home range. This range is only about 1 square mile (2.6 sq km) of land. Gila monsters come out of hiding more often in the cooler parts of the day—if they come out at all.

What a Wild Life!

Gila monsters smell with their tongue.

Gila monsters move slowly even when hunting, but they can act quickly when they need to.

11

A MIGHTY BITE

There are only two kinds of venomous lizards in North America—and the Gila monster is one of them. In order to use its venom, a Gila monster bites, using its strong jaws to hold on tight. The venom flows out into the wound mixed with the lizard's spit. It can cause a lot of pain.

A Gila monster uses its venom more as a **defense** than a way to catch and kill **prey**. So, it doesn't need to make and store a lot in its body.

What a Wild Life!
A Gila monster's bite is strong enough to kill an animal even without venom.

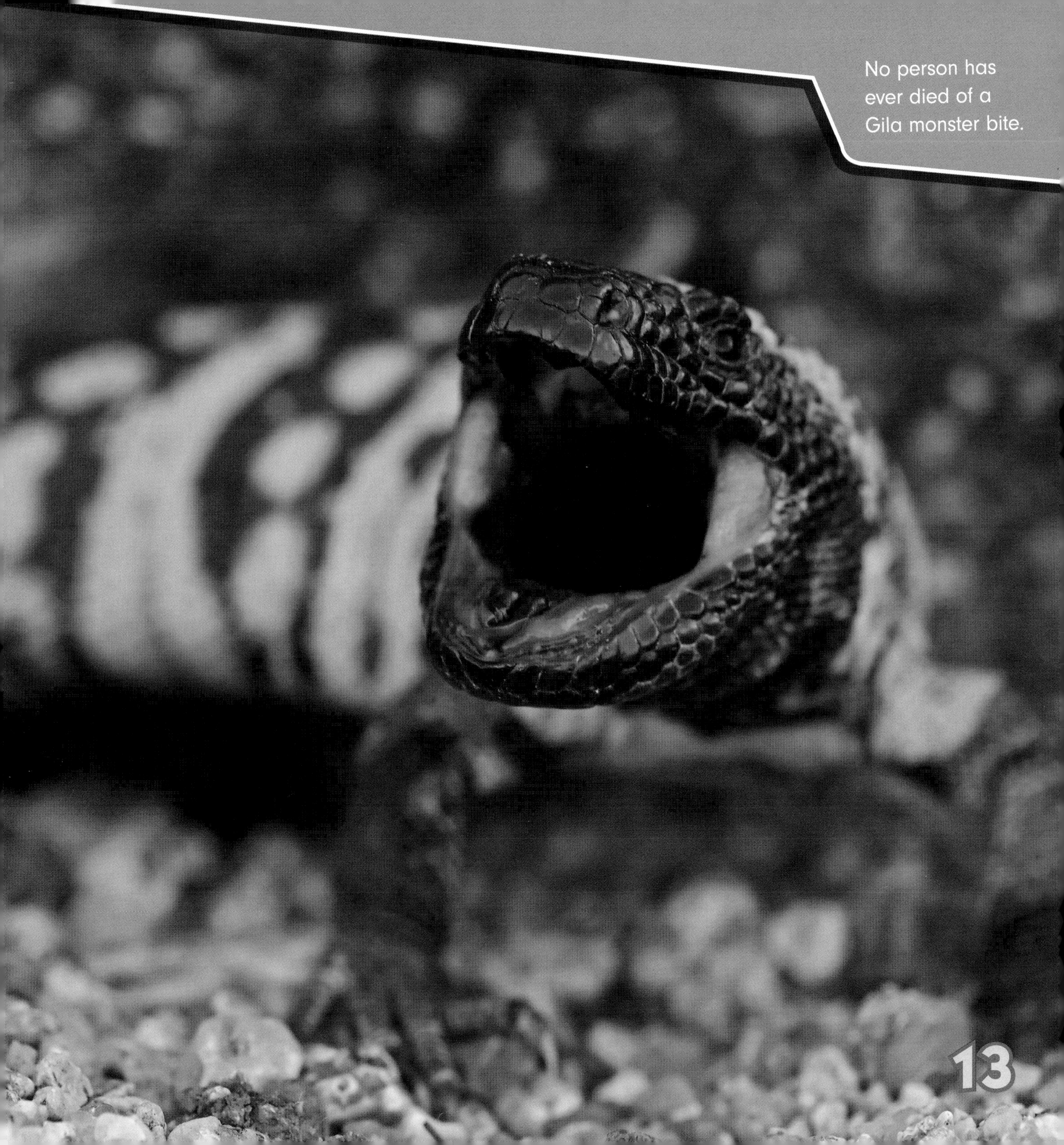

No person has ever died of a Gila monster bite.

CHOW DOWN

Gila monsters have a pretty wild meal plan. Some only eat five times a year! They eat 30 to 50 percent of their body weight at a single meal. Much of this is stored in their body and tail as fat to use later, such as during the winter.

Frogs, bugs, and birds are all part of the Gila monster **diet**. They use their claws to dig up bird and reptile eggs. They eat small animals such as mice, too.

What a Wild Life!

Few animals prey on Gila monsters. Their bright colors warn predators of their venomous bite.

15

LITTLE MONSTERS

In the spring, males fight each other for the chance to mate with females. Sometimes, they bite each other! After mating, female Gila monsters lay up to 12 eggs. When the baby Gila monsters hatch about 10 months later, they look like tiny copies of their parents. Gila monsters are the only lizards that often "overwinter" their eggs. This means that the eggs are laid in late summer or fall but don't hatch until spring.

What a Wild Life!
Gila monster venom doesn't hurt other Gila monsters.

17

SAVE THE GILA!

As people build houses and roads in the southwestern United States, Gila monsters' **habitat** is destroyed. If this continues to happen, they could become an **endangered** species.

Some people value Gila monsters because they're not often seen. They try to catch them to sell or keep as pets. In all the states where Gila monsters live, it's illegal to catch or kill them. While these laws protect Gila monsters from some human actions, they don't keep their wild habitat safe.

What a Wild Life!

When left alone, Gila monsters can live 20 to 30 years in the wild.

SUPER SPIT

Perhaps the wildest thing about Gila monsters is their spit! Scientists discovered that matter in the mix of Gila monster spit and venom helps people with the disease diabetes. Fortunately, they've learned how to make it in a lab so they don't need to have caged Gila monsters to get the matter.

Do you want to see a Gila monster? Your local zoo might have one living in its reptile house! Now that you know they're not monsters, you can have fun checking out these large lizards.

Wild Facts!

As a Gila monster gets older, the pattern on its skin will change and become special to that Gila monster.

The Apache believed that a Gila monster's breath could kill a person.

A Gila monster can go a year between meals if it needs to.

Gila monsters hibernate in the winter. That means they rest and aren't very active for several months.

Gila monsters have a forked tongue, like snakes.

GLOSSARY

burrow: a hole made by an animal in which it lives or hides

defense: a way of guarding against an enemy

diet: the food an animal eats

endangered: in danger of dying out

habitat: the natural place where an animal or plant lives

mate: to come together to make babies

predator: an animal that hunts other animals for food

prey: an animal that is hunted by other animals for food

reptile: an animal covered with scales or plates that breathes air, has a backbone, and lays eggs, such as a turtle, snake, lizard, or crocodile

reticulated: covered with crisscrossing lines, like a net

venomous: able to produce a liquid called venom that is harmful to other animals

FOR MORE INFORMATION

Books

Clark, Willow. *Gila Monster!* New York, NY: Windmill Books, 2011.

Murray, Julie. *Slowest Animals.* Edina, MN: ABDO, 2010.

Websites

Creature Features: Gila Monsters

kids.nationalgeographic.com/kids/animals/creaturefeature/gila-monsters

Check out lots of facts, a video, and pictures of this wild reptile.

Reptiles: Gila Monster

www.sandiegozoo.org/animalbytes/t-gila_monster.html

Learn more cool facts about the Gila monster.

INDEX